SOCIALISM

Xina M. Uhl and Jesse Jarnow

rosen publishing's
rosen
central®

New York

Published in 2020 by The Rosen Publishing Group, Inc.
29 East 21st Street, New York, NY 10010

Copyright © 2020 by The Rosen Publishing Group, Inc.

First Edition

Library of Congress Cataloging-in-Publication Data

Names: Uhl, Xina M., author. | Jarnow, Jesse, author.
Title: Socialism / Xina M. Uhl and Jesse Jarnow.
Description: First edition. | New York : Rosen Central, 2020. | Series: Examining political systems | Includes bibliographical references and index.
Identifiers: LCCN 2018019748| ISBN 9781508185291 (library bound) | ISBN 9781508185284 (pbk.)
Subjects: LCSH: Socialism—Juvenile literature. | Communism—Juvenile literature.
Classification: LCC HX36 .U395 2020 | DDC 335—dc23
LC record available at https://lccn.loc.gov/2018019748

Manufactured in the United States of America

On the cover: Bernie Sanders (*left*), candidate in the 2016 presidential race, has declared himself a Democratic Socialist. Karl Marx's *Das Kapital* (*upper right*) is one of the first Socialist works. A Cuban crowd holds up signs showing Che Guevara (*lower right)*, a Socialist revolutionary.

CONTENTS

Socialism refers to a planned economic system in which the government owns the four factors of production, or land, labor, capital goods, and entrepreneurship. Socialism arose from the same roots as Communism, with the publication of *The Communist Manifesto* by Karl Marx and Friedrich Engels. Both Socialism and Communism served as reaction to the excesses of capitalism, or the political and economic system in which private individuals control trade and industry instead of the government. In capitalism, profit is the motive of industry. Capitalism performs on the assumption that the basis of private enterprise is self-interest. People compete with one another for goods, services, business, and so on because it is in their self-interest to do so.

Modern Socialism occurs within a democratically elected government. The notion of cooperation among individuals forms the basis of this system. Karl Marx, in his "Critique of the Gotha Program," describes it as: "From each according to his ability, to each according to his contribution." The idea is that each person in society receives a share of the production depending on how much each has contributed. This provides the motivation to work harder and longer for more resources. The share of funds each person receives is reduced by payments for services that support the common good, such as roadways, the military, education, and health care.

This notion of a fairer, more worker-centric society would, in an ideal world, eliminate the poor, sick, and hungry. No one would be rich and

This Burmese Socialist propaganda postcard dates from around 1963. The card shows the unification of the military, represented by the soldier; farms, represented by the man with the sickle; and industry, represented by the factory worker with a hammer.

harmony would exist. The problem is that the world is not an ideal place. In the early twentieth century, Russian revolutionaries who attempted to put Marx's ideas into practice went too far in controlling the population. Starvation, economic distress, war, and tyranny followed. So did a decades-long struggle called the Cold War against capitalist and democratic nations like the United States. Eventually, the Soviet Union (USSR) dissolved under the weight of economic problems.

Labor unions such as the Industrial Workers of the World (IWW) asserted workers' powers by advocating for better conditions, pay, and hours. The unions staged strikes and held demonstrations. Long an advocate for the common man, they continue to press for a more equal distribution of wealth amongst the upper and lower classes.

In Socialism, the underlying foundation of cooperation as motivation to work, produce, and provide ignores the human tendency toward self-interest and does not reward innovation like capitalism does. However, the lack of necessary services and basic justice for those in society who struggle with poverty, illness, and other difficulties reveals a flaw in a system based solely on capitalism.

The following pages trace the history of Socialism from its beginnings through its fiery, difficult youth to its modern form in countries around the world, including the United States.

CHAPTER 1

THE BEGINNING OF SOCIALISM

The Industrial Revolution that started in England in the early eighteenth century caused massive change to industry with the development of steam engines and factories. Just as massive was the change to society. The centers of industry—cities—attracted an ever-growing population, and with that growth came problems.

Efficient factories changed the way people worked, which, in turn, changed the way people lived. Where skilled artisans had previously manufactured the bulk of the world's goods, machines such as automatic looms were beginning to take their places. Seeking employment, people flocked to cities. A new poverty emerged in factory towns. If factories were making more products, better and faster than before, then why were so many people living under such horrible conditions? The Industrial Revolution created problems that would need solutions.

A WORLDLY PARADISE

Some of the men and women who tried to tackle these problem were called utopians. They sought ways to turn the world into a utopia, a paradise—or, barring that, a better, more humane place. Often their ideas were far-fetched, but frequently they held elements worth exploring.

THREE SOCIALISTS

Three men—Charles Fourier, Henri Saint-Simon, and Robert Owen—formulated vastly different solutions to society's problems. Fourier and Saint-Simon were French. Owen was British. What

separated the three men from other utopians was the way their versions of utopia related to the modern world.

Industry was expanding. There was an ever-increasing gap between factory owners and factory workers. The new Socialists suggested that the people who worked in them might own the factories as well. This fundamental change in approach rippled outward. The utopians began to envision new ways to structure society. Unlike previous utopian thinkers, the new utopians attempted to

Robert Owen (1771–1858) was a labor reformer whose innovations inspired changes in British labor laws. He was a pioneer of British Socialism.

achieve a paradise that had little to do with God, the doctrine of original sin, or a return to Eden. Everything they needed was before them.

ROBERT OWEN AND NEW LANARK

Robert Owen was born in 1771. By the time he was nineteen, he was the superintendent of a cotton mill. Gradually, he developed his truly radical worldview.

Owen was an atheist, or someone who did not believe in God. He believed that a person's destiny was his or her own. People had to change their attitudes in order to succeed. A psychological revolution was needed, he said. Better

This 1820 engraving depicts the Scottish village of New Lanark, established by Robert Owen in 1800. The village emphasized citizens' welfare as much as commercial profit.

environments would make for better people. He outlined his ideas in a book called *A New View of Society* (1813). He advocated small, self-sufficient communities.

Owen had a chance to test his theories in the British town of New Lanark. In 1800, he set up a model factory and a model village. He made sure that working and living conditions were excellent. Owen paid specific detail to education. The factory's earnings funded the school. New Lanark was a wild success. The factory turned a huge profit. More important, the workers were happy. Owen established many reforms. Most workers in England worked thirteen or fourteen hours a day. The men and women in Owen's factories only worked ten and a half hours.

Owen's financial backers thought he was spending too much money. They wanted less money put back into the community and more money given to investors. Eventually, Owen broke his ties with them. He founded several other cooperative communities throughout England and one in the United States. Although Owen's communities eventually failed, he still had a positive effect on the country's working conditions. From 1802 to 1891, the British parliament passe eight Factory Acts based on Owen's ideas.

HENRI SAINT-SIMON SEEKS HARMONY

Meanwhile, in France, Henri Saint-Simon was championing his own ideas. Born in 1760, Saint-Simon fought with the colonists in the American Revolution. He made a small fortune in investments during the French Revolution. He celebrated the triumph of industry. Science, he thought, should guide society. It should aid religion, not replace it. He imagined that scientists and industrialists would be the leaders of the new society.

Saint-Simon collected his work into *Social Organization: The Science of Man*. His predictions proved particularly accurate. He foretold of a world in which politics and economics became a fluid whole. Oddly enough, in the past fifty years, this has come to be true. However, it has not happened in the way Saint-Simon would have liked. Saint-Simon thought that economic leaders could carefully plan production for the good of the people. For Saint-Simon, the goal was not profit, but harmony.

Gradually, Saint-Simon developed a cult of followers. As a movement, the Saint-Simonians advocated many of the causes that more mature forms of Socialism would embrace. They wished to abolish inheritance rights. They believed that workers should control the means of production. They wanted to give women more rights under the law. The Saint-Simonians were never able to put their theory into practice. After Saint-Simon died, the movement deteriorated into a religious cult. It soon succumbed to petty bickering and dissolved.

CHARLES FOURIER'S UNIVERSAL ANALOGY

Perhaps the most influential of the early Socialists was Charles Fourier. He was easily the most optimistic (if most unrealistic) of the eighteenth-century Socialists. Like Saint-Simon, Fourier was French. He witnessed the French Revolution firsthand from his home in the provinces. He saw what industrialization had done to society. Unlike Saint-Simon, he did not embrace science and industry. He thought that by being forced into menial tasks, workers were becoming less able to think and reason.

Fourier presented a complete and exacting model for a new society, down to the most microscopic details. He planned different jobs for each member of his society, attempting to balance them carefully. Fourier's *Theory of Social Organization*, published in 1820, was a massive work. It revealed the inner workings of a brilliant, if troubled, mind.

This 1865 illustration from an Italian newspaper shows a crowded, miserable homeless shelter in London, an unpleasant side effect of industrialization.

Fourier's work centered on his fervent belief in what he called Universal Analogy. Everything was connected, he thought. The physical world was an exact representation of the physical and spiritual laws of the universe. And everything reflected human nature. Fourier believed that his work followed logically from Sir Isaac Newton's laws of gravitation. While Newton showed why physical objects were attracted to each other, Fourier attempted to do the same with the human spirit.

Fourier formulated his theory of attraction based on a detailed list of distinct personality types comprised of passions. His theory outlined twelve passions that must be satisfied for people to be happy. To attain this, he suggested a precise arrangement of personality types that would counterbalance each other. When this formula was followed, Fourier believed, harmony would be created with the universe. He called his paradise Harmony. Fourier planned to accomplish this through a series of communities called phalanxes.

Each phalanx would be a rigorously planned community. To Fourier, if people enjoyed their work, they would do it well. Jobs would be assigned based on the passions. Everything would fall into place around this. Fourier believed in his theories with an unwavering faith. He attracted his share of followers, though they were never able to raise the money to build an actual phalanx.

Fourier spent many years searching for financial backers. The broad scope of Fourier's project confused many potential followers. Where they were likely to be excited by one of his ideas, they were equally likely to be put off by others.

Many of Fourier's writings about Harmony closely resembled science fiction. Once the world adopted his systems, the average lifespan would increase to 144 years and humans would develop tails. The polar ice caps would melt, and the seas around the North Pole would be turned into "a kind of lemonade." Man's enemies in the animal kingdom would become his allies, turning into such things as anticrocodiles and antisharks.

In short, Charles Fourier lived in a dream world. But it was a dream that ultimately had a positive effect on many people. Almost forty years after Fourier's death in 1837, Friedrich Engels wrote of him lovingly in *Socialism: Utopian and Scientific*, calling his work "masterly."

A NINETEENTH-CENTURY AMERICAN COMMUNE

In 1841, George Ripley founded Brook Farm in Massachusetts. He based his community on a combination of Fourier's teachings and those of the transcendentalist Henry David Thoreau. Likewise, a direct line can be drawn from Fourier, Owen, and Saint-Simon to the kibbutz movement in Israel. In the 1960s and '70s, communes became popular in the United States. Many idealistic young men and women moved to communes to escape the pressures of modern life. In a sense, they agreed with Fourier. They wanted to be active in all aspects of their lives, not just their highly specialized jobs. Though most of the communes closed after several years, some still thrive.

Owen, Saint-Simon, and Fourier provided the starting point for Karl Marx and Friedrich Engels's plans for widespread Socialist change. But where Marx and Engels would eventually call for statewide evolution, Owen, Saint-Simon, and Fourier favored small settlements. It was easier, they thought, to affect a more controlled group of people. In this way, they were direct influences on hundreds of utopian communes and compounds that were founded across the globe. (A commune is a small community, usually based around a farm. People who lived there shared possessions and jobs.)

THE KIBBUTZ

Many have argued that Socialism would work on a small scale. Throughout much of the twentieth century, this was proved

This photo from around 1935 depicts Jewish women plowing a field by hand in a kibbutz in what would become Israel.

mostly true by a network of kibbutzim in Israel. A kibbutz is a small collective settlement. Residents divide the work equally and share larger possessions (such as cars). The average kibbutz has several hundred inhabitants. The population is generally made up of young Israelis, traveling students, and transient workers. Some have said that the kibbutzim are the closest people have come to living the principles laid out by Charles Fourier. To some, kibbutzim feel very much like summer camps with more chores.

The first kibbutz was founded in 1910. After 1948, kibbutzim played an important part in the settlement of Israel, forming the basis of small autonomous communities. For the most part, they are self-sufficient. Each kibbutz is arranged like a village. There is a library, a grocery, a laundry, and other services. There are few cars, and most residents walk or ride bicycles. Politically, a kibbutz is a direct democracy. Every member has a vote in each policy decision. Small committees deal with day-to-day planning on a variety of matters.

The residents of the kibbutz do a wide range of jobs. They are responsible for maintaining the settlement by doing chores. Kibbutzim make up an important part of Israel's agricultural output. Members harvest food for both themselves and others. Many kibbutzim also have industrial components to them. They manufacture a variety of products in small factories, including electric motors, irrigation systems, and clothing. Kibbutzim exist within a larger capitalist system. In recent years, this has led kibbutzim to change and evolve. There is more of an emphasis on the individual now. But, for the most part, they retain their basic principles. The kibbutz still takes care of the housing, food, health care, and education of its inhabitants. Likewise, the means of production are still owned and controlled by the workers. Many kibbutzim supplement their incomes by offering bed-and-breakfast hotels. Many also have museums.

CHAPTER 2

THE COMMUNIST MANIFESTO

As the nineteenth century progressed, Europe experienced growing poverty and unrest. Socialism held growing appeal. The utopian Fourier had opposed economic system based on private ownership known as capitalism. But a new kind of Socialist emerged, led by Karl Marx and Friedrich Engels.

Marx was a German historian. Engels was born in Prussia, the son of a textile magnate. When he was young, Engels had gone to England to help his father manage his business. While he was there,

Karl Marx is widely acknowledged as the founder of Socialism. The son of a German lawyer, he studied law, history, and philosophy before becoming the political editor of a radical German newspaper.

he observed the conditions of the towns, the factories, and the people. He published his findings in a book. Shortly after, he began to write for a magazine that Marx edited. In 1844, in Paris, the two met in person. Their meeting was the beginning of a relationship that would last until Marx died in 1883.

Both Marx and Engels belonged to the Communist League. In the nineteenth century, the word "Communist" meant something vastly different than what it came to imply later. For Marx and Engels, "Communism" and "Socialism" were interchangeable terms. So it was in 1847 when they drafted one of the most influential political documents in modern history, *The Communist Manifesto*.

Communist Manifesto

By KARL MARX and
FREDERICK ENGELS

Workingmen of all countries, unite!
You have nothing to lose but your chains.
You have a world to win.

Price 5 Cents

CHARLES H. KERR & COMPANY
-349 E. Ohio St.   Chicago, Ill.

A CALL TO ARMS

The Communist Manifesto was divided into four parts. The first two of these are the most important. Part one outlines Marx and Engels's conception of history. Part two explains their plan for the present. Part three presents a detailed catalogue of different kinds of Socialism. Finally, part four closes with a brief summary of the world situation and an enthusiastic call to arms.

An English version of *The Communist Manifesto* prints the famous phrase "Workingmen of all countries, unite!" on the cover. See page 51 for a partial transcription.

CLASS STRUGGLES AND CAPITALISM

Marx and Engels emphasized teleology, the belief that history was working inevitably toward a final product. All of history, they said, was the result of class struggle, between those who labored and those who controlled labor. Under feudalism, vassals and serfs worked in exchange for land and protection from lords. It was a highly controlled system. People could not work for themselves.

Feudalism gave way naturally to capitalism, in which men were free to conduct business any way they wanted. If people worked for themselves, productivity was bound to increase. Free competition would lead to monopoly, Marx and Engels suggested. Monopolies would lead to price-fixing in which consumers would pay more for goods and services. What would begin with the ideal of complete freedom would perversely end with corporate totalitarianism. In this prediction, Marx and Engels were absolutely right. It occurred time and time again in their day, and it continues to happen today.

Marx and Engels believed that this consolidation would also be capitalism's downfall. For starters, there would be a much greater divide between the classes. The factory owners who controlled the means of production were known as the bourgeoisie. The workers who toiled in factories were known as the proletariat. As time went on, the rich would get richer and the poor would get poorer.

However, the proletariat was now relatively centralized since its members all worked in factories. They would organize by forming unions and workers' organizations. And, once they organized, they would overthrow the bourgeoisie.

A WORKERS' REVOLUTION

Marx and Engels began to call for revolution. In their world, the idea of revolution was not so far-fetched. Fifty years earlier, a series of revolts had taken place in France. Only three years before, weavers in Germany had attacked the homes of factory owners. Living conditions were horrible. Famines occurred throughout Europe, driving up food prices. In some cities, there were riots over the high cost of bread and potatoes. Meanwhile, wages dropped to an all-time low. If there was any time and place ripe for revolution, it was Europe in the mid-nineteenth century.

In *The Communist Manifesto*, Marx and Engels dealt with the specifics of what they wanted to achieve. Their goals ranged from personal to governmental. Like Saint-Simon, they believed that change in society could only come with a broad shift in thinking. They wanted to liberate society from the psychological shackles imposed on it by capitalism.

The first step, they wrote, was universal suffrage. Everybody should have the right to vote, from people of the proletariat to members of the bourgeoisie. In addition, Marx and Engels wished to ban private property. By "private property," they did not mean personal goods but property on a larger scale, such as factories. Industry would be placed in the hands of the government. And, with the government (theoretically) controlled by the people, the government would enter the Socialist stage. Eventually, they predicted, mechanisms of the old class tensions would fall away, and a true Communist (or classless) state would be achieved. In nondemocratic countries, they called for revolution. "Working men of the world, unite!" they wrote.

DAS KAPITAL

Marx and Engels worked tirelessly to present their vision to the world. They traveled the world, making speeches and helping workers organize. Both men also wrote prolifically. They were tireless historians.

Das Kapital, Karl Marx's stinging criticism of capitalism, is widely seen to be Marx's most significant work. See page 52 for a partial transcription.

Their writings were twofold. Because they wished to convert the world to their vision, they analyzed the world's current situation as well as its history.

In 1867, Marx published *Das Kapital* (Capital). It was the first of a proposed three volumes, which would present his critique of capitalism. Unfortunately, Marx died in 1883 before he could complete the second and third volumes. Engels wrote two more volumes of *Das Kapital* and continued to edit Marx's work (as well as his own) until his death in 1895.

SOCIALISM IN GOVERNMENT

There has never been a fully functional example of Marx and Engels's work. Several countries purported to be Socialist, including the former Soviet Union, though they weren't. In each case, the fledgling governments took some elements of Socialism, while disregarding its fundamental aspects. They twisted them into varieties of totalitarianism.

Das Kapital.

Kritik der politischen Oekonomie.

Von

Karl Marx.

Erster Band.

Buch I: Der Produktionsprocess des Kapitals.

Das Recht der Uebersetzung wird vorbehalten.

Hamburg
Verlag von Otto Meissner.
1867.

New-York: L. W. Schmidt. 24 Barclay-Street.

DYSTOPIAN FICTION

In literature, trends come and go. Dystopian fiction (a dystopia is the opposite of a utopia) is a popular trend set to continue growing through the 2020s. A mainstay of young adult (YA) fiction, it includes novels about dark, oppressive societies from the perspective of a teenager. Examples are *The Hunger Games, Divergent,* and *The Maze Runner. The Giver* by Lois Lowry is a 1993 bestseller said to have begun the teenager-centric style of dystopian YA. However, the roots of dystopian novels go back further, to George Orwell's classic *1984* (written in 1949), which is the story of a single man's battle against a dehumanizing society. Similar books include Aldous Huxley's *Brave New World,* Ray Bradbury's *Fahrenheit 451*, and Franz Kafka's *The Trial*. These works grew out of Socialism in several ways. The authors were attempting to answer many of the same questions as Karl Marx. They raised important issues about an individual's place in society. They considered what contribution a person should make. They pondered the role of the government. In the process, they critiqued both Socialism and capitalism. If pushed to their extremes, Socialism and capitalism resembled each other in their fascism. The books revealed the similar human impulses behind both systems and encourage readers to take a closer look at the world in which they live. Dystopian works push readers to value and protect the freedoms that they have by showing them what life would be without them.

THE SOVIETS

The former Union of Soviet Socialist Republics (USSR) came closest to Socialism. Following a series of revolutions beginning in 1917, the Russian government began to socialize. Sadly, they

This Soviet commemorative poster celebrates the sixtieth anniversary of the October Revolution. The poster depicts Communists over-throwing the old world, marked by exploitation and inequality.

held many of Marx's writings as absolute doctrine. They did not adapt them to their situation as they needed to. Marx was placed on a pedestal. His work became law instead of simple theory.

Under the leadership of Vladimir Lenin, and then Josef Stalin, they put the nation's farms under state control. Unfortunately, they often made the farmers serve the interests of the army and the cities at the expense of rural residents. This put an undue strain on the country's farmers who didn't have enough to eat.

In addition, the government (especially under Stalin) was ruthless and cruel, frequently murdering those who attempted dissent. While the country was, in fact, socialized, it was never

This photo shows Russian exiles in Siberia. Siberia has been used since the seventeenth century as a place of exile and forced labor camps for the political enemies of Russian rulers.

placed in the hands of the proletariat. There were some positive aspects to the socialization of the Soviet Union. Literacy rates improved vastly. Medical coverage became almost universal. Unfortunately, these came at great expense. Civil liberties were severely curtailed.

The government controlled production and the media. The right to dissent was quashed. This is one of the primary problems of large-scale Socialism. Not everyone wants to participate, and the Soviet Union was particularly forceful. Many of those who resisted were sent to the desolate tundra of Siberia. The country continued to place industry before agriculture, and a series of famines hit the Soviet Union hard. By the early 1990s, Communism had entirely collapsed in the USSR.

THE NAZIS

Likewise, following World War I, the German government fell under a program of so-called National Socialism (Nazi, for short) under the leadership of Adolf Hitler. The party's version of Socialism began somewhat close to Marx's original notion, though it was gradually perverted. Where Marx had emphasized class struggle as the logical engine of history, the Nazis claimed that racial strife defined the past.

With evolutionary scientist Charles Darwin as their model, the Nazis instituted a program of genocide. They attempted to create a pure race of people called the Aryans. They separated non-Aryans, detaining and killing them. Their victims included Jews, Gypsies, and gays.

Although Nazi Germany was socialized to a degree, it left

This photo from 1933 shows Adolf Hitler, the Nazi leader, giving the fascist salute at a meeting. Hitler would go on to conduct one of the most devastating genocides of all time.

industrial ownership in private hands. The Nazis worked with factory owners to control the economy. The country adopted expansionist policies during the 1930s and '40s, invading several countries, and beginning World War II.

While Marx and Engels's brand of Socialism was never truly instituted, *The Communist Manifesto* spread throughout the world. It was translated into dozens of languages. It found its way into the hands of thousands of workers, organizers, and scholars, having perhaps a larger impact on the shape of world history than any other political document of modern times.

CHAPTER 3

UNIONS, TRADE, AND SOCIALISM

America's industrial workers experienced the same discontent as their fellows in Europe. Workers formed small unions at first, but these unions increased in size and number over time.

THE IWW

From the start, there were struggles between worker organizations in the United States. The American Federation of Labor (AFL) was one major group. Another was the Industrial Workers of the World (IWW). Members of this group came to be known as the Wobblies (sometimes shortened to Wob), though nobody is quite sure why. The groups clashed with each other over many issues. The AFL was comprised primarily of craft unions. The IWW had a more industrial base. By 1905, the IWW had emerged as the predominant force in the American labor movement. Its attitude was deeply influenced by *The Communist Manifesto*.

This photo from 1914 shows a crowd of IWW members demonstrating against violence in the Colorado coal strike. The gathering took place in New York City's Union Square.

Led by Eugene Debs, the Wobblies laid out a much clearer vision of how to achieve its means. It presented its vision in the constitution of the Industrial Workers of the World in Chicago in 1905. The vision was called syndicalism. The first step would be to create a general union. The union would create a network of workers spread across the nation. It would bind the country's proletariat together.

Gradually, the workers would stage strikes. Eventually, there would be a general strike. The workers would have the power to stop the nation in its tracks. Once they did this, they could achieve what they wanted. They could negotiate better hours, more humane conditions, and higher pay. Within the framework of the United States, they would reorganize. Instead of the capitalists at the center, the workers would now be in control. Not only would they provide the means for a nonviolent revolution, but they would also provide a structure for the society that would come to exist afterward.

FIGHTING FOR FREE SPEECH

After internal struggles, the IWW initiated one of its first national fights in 1907. It was for free speech. A simple way for the group to attract new members was to deliver speeches on street corners. Time and time again, police harassed the speakers. Despite the fact that their right to gather and speak was protected by the Constitution, many towns passed anti-IWW ordinances. To combat this, hundreds of Wobblies would descend on a town and begin to agitate on dozens of street corners. Police would arrest them. Soon, the jailed Wobblies would overwhelm the town's legal system, and the local government would be forced to repeal the ordinances.

The first major strike the IWW organized took place in the mining town of McKees Rocks, Pennsylvania, in 1907. The town, outside of Pittsburgh, was a mining community. When factory owners tried to institute a new wage system, a committee of forty workers questioned them. The workers were immediately fired. Quickly, the miners went on strike. For two months, they remained steadfast. They battled state troopers. Many were injured, and several people were killed. Eventually, the company relented and returned to the old wage system.

VICTORIES AND FAILURES

The IWW's biggest victory took place in Lawrence, Massachusetts, in 1912. Without warning, factory owners cut pay by thirty-two cents a week. In those days, thirty-two cents was enough to buy ten loaves of bread. Word spread quickly.

In less than twenty-four hours, factories throughout Lawrence had called sympathy strikes. "Better to starve fighting than to starve working!" the strikers chanted. The strike lasted for nine long, cold weeks. The battles were vicious. Local police shot fire hoses filled with freezing water at the picket lines. The more brutal the opposition, the more determined the workers were to continue. In March, nearly three months after the strike began, the employers agreed to give the workers pay raises.

The IWW also won victories in other factory towns, such as Paterson, New Jersey, and Akron, Ohio. Unfortunately, the methods that allowed them such great triumphs also sowed the seeds of their eventual failure. Strikes were direct action. Goals could be achieved quickly. Unfortunately, once the strikes were over, the IWW often failed to organize the workers on a more permanent basis. Within a year, there was little union organization left in Lawrence, for example. Still, the influence of the IWW was widespread. It inspired countless local workers to organize.

The existence of the IWW had always been shaky. It was opposed by people and groups on all fronts. From within, great factions formed. Some members of the IWW—mostly from the eastern part of the country—continued to advocate syndicalism. Others, mostly from the West, were more inclined towards anarchy. The anarchists distrusted political power. They were suspicious of any attempts to organize on a broad scale. They were also more inclined toward using violent tactics to achieve their goals. By 1914, the anarchists had alienated many of the left-wing politicians who might otherwise have supported the IWW.

The IWW continued to be persecuted by police groups and right-wing politicians throughout the nation. Joe Hill, a popular musician who wrote many songs about the IWW cause, was accused of murder and executed in 1915. Frank Little, a fiery organizer who was half American Indian, was lynched in 1917.

As World War I loomed, many workers focused their energies on the enemy overseas, forgetting about class struggles on the home front. They continued to organize strikes. Some IWW members were accused of treason and for being under the influence of the Germans. However, the IWW never made a formal statement against the war.

In September 1917, 165 IWW leaders were arrested and charged with obstruction of the government's war program. The next year, 101 of these men and women were brought before the famous Chicago judge, Kenesaw Mountain Landis. The trial lasted through the hot summer months of 1918. The IWW attempted to prove that their interests lay in improving the conditions of working people. Landis would not allow much of their evidence, saying that it was irrelevant. The

Federal Judge Kenesaw Mountain Landis is best known as the first commissioner of organized professional baseball. His name came from the mountain where his father was wounded during the Civil War.

members of the IWW were convicted and punished to varying degrees, ranging from imprisonment to fines. It was the effective end of the IWW.

PROGRESSIVE REFORMS

As the American government was oppressing the IWW, it was entering what became known as the Progressive Era. Many reforms were enacted under Presidents Theodore Roosevelt and Woodrow Wilson. The laws regulated the United States's thriving industries. Companies were becoming huge. They were turning into monopolies, or trusts—vast corporations that cornered the markets, eliminated the competition, and controlled prices. While this strategy was good for big companies, it was bad for small companies, because they couldn't compete.

Roosevelt became known as a "trust-buster." The Federal Trade Commission was established with the specific purpose of regulating businesses that operated in multiple states. This was only the tip of the iceberg, though. Dozens of laws were passed. The laws did very little to actually change anything on a fundamental level,

THE JUNGLE

UPTON SINCLAIR

An early copy of Upton Sinclair's *The Jungle* is shown above. The book caused such a furor that President Theodore Roosevelt read its graphic, unsettling descriptions and supported legislation to regulate the food industry.

but they were clearly rooted in Socialist ideals. They were framed with the average citizen in mind.

In addition to strikes, journalists called muckrakers began publishing investigative reports in which they revealed the scandalous practices of huge corporations. Upton Sinclair's 1906 novel *The Jungle*, for example, looked closely at the meatpacking industry in Chicago. This led to the creation of both the Meat Inspection Act and the Pure Food and Drug Act. The Interstate Commerce Commission was formed as a result of the Mann-Elkins Act when abuses in telephone and telegraph industries were uncovered. The government also began to control the country's money and banking systems more tightly after passing the Federal Reserve Act. Meanwhile, governmental commissions were organized to investigate social ills.

THE JUNGLE AND SOCIALISM

Upton Sinclair's novel *The Jungle* revolves around two Lithuanian immigrants to Chicago who experience the poor working conditions in the meatpacking yards for which the city was famous.

Sinclair became a Socialist by 1903 and contributed regularly to Socialist newspaper *Appeal to Reason* when the editor asked him to write a novel about wage slavery and provided him with a $500 advance. Sinclair disguised himself and did seven weeks of research into the meatpacking industry. Armed with this research, he wrote and serialized the book in *Appeal to Reason*. Afterward, he compiled it into a novel. It was rejected by five publishers until Doubleday accepted it. Graphic scenes such as the following caused an uproar among the public.

(continued on the next page)

(continued from the previous page)

> There were cattle which had been fed on "whiskey-malt," the refuse of the breweries, and had become what the men called "steerly" — which means covered with boils. It was a nasty job killing these, for when you plunged your knife into them they would burst and splash foul-smelling stuff into your face; and when a man's sleeves were smeared with blood, and his hands steeped in it, how was he ever to wipe his face, or to clear his eyes so that he could see?

The sales of US meat plummeted after the book's publication, and even President Theodore Roosevelt heard about the scandalous claims it included. Attention from the president and Congress quickly resulted in legislation designed to improve the quality of food in the country.

Many states passed laws that placed limits on how many hours a week people were allowed to work. Two constitutional amendments were proposed and passed. The Sixteenth Amendment instituted a graduated income tax. The Seventeenth Amendment allowed citizens to vote for senators in direct elections. Previously, they had been chosen by state legislatures.

Though the reforms never went as far as the IWW wanted, they were a start. And they were a direct result of the public uprisings in the early years of the twentieth century. In a number of ways, these reforms were attempts to keep the Socialist movement under control. President Roosevelt frequently worked in concert with representatives of industry in order to pass laws.

The United States's economy was large and unruly. It was experiencing some of the biggest and most uncontrolled growth spurts it had ever known. Regulation was good for all parties involved. Roosevelt was able to please both the public and big business concerns. These kinds of reforms continued until the beginning of World War II. Their peak came with President Franklin Delano Roosevelt's Works Progress Administration in the late 1930s. His programs distributed money and services to underprivileged people across America. More important, the programs created work for thousands of Americans who were suffering from the effects of the Great Depression.

CHAPTER 4

SOCIALISM AROUND THE WORLD

In the years following World War II, Socialists around the world reconsidered their positions. The world had changed. The failures of Communist Russia were clear. So were the successes of capitalist, democratic United States.

To Marx and Engels, Socialism and Communism were basically the same thing. Yet as the Communist movement grew, it soon became clear that there was a division between those who insisted that the Communist revolution had to be forced through violent means and those who felt that it could be achieved through the democratic process. The differences between the two groups widened once the world had seen the Soviet experiment.

At a convention held in Frankfurt, Germany, in 1951, Socialist International, an umbrella association of international Socialist organizations, distanced itself from Communism in a document called the Frankfurt Declaration. It said, in part:

> has split the International Labour Movement and has
> set back the realisation of Socialism in many countries

for decades. Communism falsely claims a share in the Socialist tradition. In fact it has distorted that tradition beyond recognition. It has built up a rigid theology which is incompatible with the critical spirit of Marxism. Where Socialists aim to achieve freedom and justice by removing the exploitation which divides men under capitalism, Communists seek to sharpen those class divisions only in order to establish the dictatorship of a single party ... Wherever it has achieved power it has destroyed freedom or the chance of gaining freedom.

In 1956, British scholar C. A. R. Crosland wrote an important book titled *The Future of Socialism*. The book evaluated Socialism's goals and compared them to the current state of the world.

SOCIALISM IN EUROPE AND CANADA

Socialism's main goal in the early twentieth century, Crosland wrote, was to create a welfare state. That is, a government that would provide for and support its citizens. Looked at from that perspective, Crosland said, Socialists had accomplished quite a lot. However, there were still several objectives yet to be achieved. Of prime importance, power had to be diffused. The upper class still dominated most countries. In addition, the standard of living needed to be raised.

BRITAIN

Crosland was a member of the Labour Party. The party was founded in 1912 but rose to prominence in the 1940s and 1950s. Crosland and his associates advocated a less revolutionary way of achieving Socialist aims within a government. They were inspired by Franklin Delano Roosevelt's sweeping social programs in America, many of which had been dismantled during

World War II. As the Labour Party came to power in Britain over the course of the 1950s and '60s, they instituted their plans, one of which was to impose environmental regulations on businesses.

Under Prime Minister Clement Attlee, the ruling Labour Party created the tax-funded National Health Service in 1948. The National Health Service was the crowning achievement of a comprehensive welfare program that made it possible for any British citizen to go to a doctor and get free treatment. Attlee's government also the Bank of England and a number of industries in order to regulate their growth. These included gas, railroad, electric utilities, coal, and the iron and steel industries.

In the 1960s, the Labour Party under Prime Minister Harold Wilson did not further the aggressive nationalization programs of Attlee. However, Wilson introduced a number of important social reforms. These included the abolishment of the death penalty and the legalization of abortion and homosexuality.

Socialism as practiced by the Labour Party in Britain, was far removed from what Karl Marx and Friedrich Engels envisioned. Socialism was Britain's utopia. Yet the Labour Party acknowledged that pure Socialism could never be fully achieved. The party also understood that most people would never be able to accept Socialism as a way of life.

In 1958, George Orwell wrote a book titled *The Road to Wigan Pier*. He examined why most working people didn't like Socialism. Orwell traveled to an industrial town in the north of England. In addition to living with miners, he descended into coal pits. He studied people with jobs and people without jobs. Examining class differences in England, he compared the working class and the upper class and discussed why they didn't like each other. Many people saw Socialism as elitist. They didn't like being told what was good for them.

What the Labour Party achieved, then, was a compromise. Throughout Europe, Socialist-influenced governments came to power and thrived. Socialist Léon Blum was the premier of France

Clement Attlee (1883–1967), leader of the British Labour Party, addresses demonstrators at a rally in Cardiff, Great Britain, on August 2, 1936. Attlee was one of the most prominent British Socialists of the twentieth century.

in 1938 and again in 1946. However, his power was checked by a powerful conservative opposition. It wasn't until the rise of François Mitterrand in the 1980s that Socialists controlled the presidency, the French Assembly, and local governments.

SWEDEN, GERMANY, AND CANADA

Sweden initiated broad policies that took care of its citizens "from the cradle to the grave." In addition to a national health care system, the Swedish enacted such comprehensive programs as maternity benefits, allowances for children, and pensions. These benefits are paid for by taxes. Germany, too, has Socialist policies, including a national health care system for its citizens.

This May 16, 2018, photo shows Canadian prime minister Justin Trudeau at a meeting in New York City. Trudeau's father, Pierre Trudeau, served as Canada's prime minister for four terms.

In Canada during the twentieth century, the Liberal Party became the most dominant political party. It has championed progressive social policies. The party instituted welfare programs under Prime Minister William Lyon Mackenzie King (1874–1950). They included a mother's allowance and an old age pension. Universal health care, government-financed student loans, the Canada Pension Plan, and the Canada Assistance Plan provide services to the public.

In 2015, Liberal Party leader Justin Trudeau was voted into office as prime minister after a decade of conservative government rule. Trudeau accused conservative government policies of benefiting the wealthy at the expense of the poor and working class. Trudeau's administration focuses on a number of causes typical of Socialists, such as racial equality, transgender rights, environmental regulations, and support of labor unions.

INDEPENDENCE AND SOCIALISM

Throughout the second half of the twentieth centuries, many countries in Africa, Asia, and the West Indies gained their independence from European colonial powers. The leaders of these movements were often attracted to Socialism. Numerous countries in Central and South America also struggled with newly

This photo, taken around 1958, shows Fidel Castro (*left*) and Che Guevara (*right*) in Havana, Cuba. Guevara, a passionate advocate of revolution through the use of guerilla warfare, was executed by the Bolivian army in 1967.

independent governments, many of which leaned toward Socialism. In 1959, revolutionary leader Fidel Castro led a successful coup against Cuban dictator General Fulgencio Batista with the help of Argentinian rebel Ernesto "Che" Guevara. Guevara became a martyr to the Communist cause when he was killed trying to export a Cuban-style government to Bolivia in 1967.

In 1965, Castro merged political parties and revolutionary groups into a single party, the Cuban Communist Party (PCC). No other political parties are allowed, and dissidents are imprisoned. The 1976 Cuban Constitution supported this system. A 2002 referendum established Socialism for good.

Cuba remains one of the only Socialist systems based on Marxist-Leninist principles.

Another variety of Socialist government took root in Africa in the 1960s. It was called villagization. Governments hoped to improve agricultural output by creating villages. In Tanzania, under President Julius Nyerere, most of the residents lived in homesteads scattered across the country. After moving them to villages, the economy improved. More important, the country's disparate tribes were united.

But this change had negative side effects, too. Under villagization, people used the land differently. While the system was similar to a network of kibbutzim, it often had a negative impact on the environment. Nyerere relented, and the government returned to a freer market.

From the 1950s through the 1980s, thirty-five African countries adopted Socialist governments. However, after the USSR collapsed in 1989, Socialism fell out of favor. Democratic governments gained power in Africa beginning in the 1990s.

TWENTY-FIRST CENTURY CHALLENGES

Venezuela's economy is based in large part on the country's reserves of oil and gas. When oil and gas are commanding high prices on the world markets, the country maintains a stable government and funding of Socialist policies like those of president Hugo Chávez, who was elected in 1998. After his death in 2013, the country struggled, and when oil prices dropped substantially in 2015, the government's state-owned gas and oil products produced less income, which caused subsidies for food and social programs to dwindle. Riots, starvation, and skyrocketing prices continue to cause significant problems for the population.

CHAPTER 5

SOCIALISM AND THE MODERN UNITED STATES

Socialism has caused much controversy over the past two centuries, especially in the United States, where capitalism is a driving force in government as well as the economy.

Despite the fact that Socialism never really caught on in the United States, it has influenced various reformers, labor activists, and civil rights activists throughout the twentieth century.

THE FRANKFURT SCHOOL

Popular culture was created by the elite to stifle the working class, or so claimed the scholars who came to

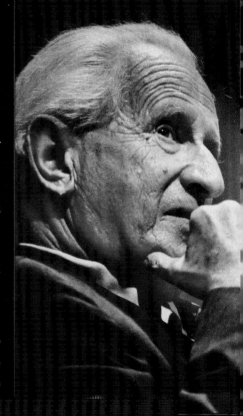

Philosopher Herbert Marcuse, a committed Marxist, appears in this 1972 photo. Marcuse called US nationalism the "most aggressive and most destructive form that exists."

be known as the Frankfurt School. They explained the lack of a Socialist revolution in the United States by its popular culture. According to these scholars' reasoning, the American working class, soothed by popular culture, did not think enough to question authority.

Herbert Marcuse was an influential member of the Frankfurt School who wrote about the state of Marxism in the rest of the world. In the late 1950s, he wrote a book titled *Soviet Marxism.* It was one of the first pro-Marxist books to heavily criticize the Soviet Union. He predicted many of the changes that would eventually lead to the collapse of Soviet Communism in the 1970s and '80s.

The impact of the Frankfurt School cannot be underestimated. The ideas of its scholars led to concepts such as multiculturalism and pluralism. They acknowledged that there was more than one version of every story. There is an old saying that "history is written by the winners." The Frankfurt School contradicted this. Until then, many schools assigned books from the established canon. They were books written by the ruling classes. After the Frankfurt School, the canon became more diverse. Teachers began teaching books that were more diverse, such as the use of slave narratives to study the Civil War.

The Frankfurt School also influenced many writers who weren't Marxists. In 1980, Howard Zinn published *A People's History of the United States*, which told the country's history from the perspective of the working class. His book was extremely popular. Zinn has revised and republished the book several times. In 1986, Noam Chomsky and Edward Herman wrote *Manufacturing Consent*. The book explored how the media serves the interests of the ruling class.

AMERICAN FOLK MUSIC AND SENATOR MCCARTHY

In 1933, John and Alan Lomax set out across America in a car with recording equipment built specially into the trunk. They wanted to use new recording devices to record American music.

Lomax made the first recordings of blues singers, gospel choirs, preachers, sharecroppers, and others. Much of the music he recorded was performed by African Americans, some of them former slaves.

(continued on the next page)

Senator Joseph McCarthy accuses an American employee of Fort Monmouth of espionage during a hearing of the House Un-American Activities Committee (HUAC) in 1941.

(continued from the previous page)

The music that Lomax recorded was called "folk music." Many people interested in folk music were also curious about Socialism.

Charles Seeger was a friend of Lomax. Seeger's son, Pete, began to sing songs in the folk tradition. As part of a group called the Weavers, Pete Seeger toured the country, selling out shows all over America. The Weavers performed songs by legendary musicians (and friends) like Woody Guthrie, Leadbelly, and others. They sang songs from cultures around the world. Their music was about the hopes and struggles of everyday people.

In the late 1940s, the Weavers had a record contract and a string of radio hits. Senator Joseph McCarthy, a Republican senator from Wisconsin, was the chair of the House Un-American Activities Committee (HUAC). He investigated and persecuted people who were suspected of having Socialist or Communist sympathies. He placed them on a blacklist, which made it hard for them to keep or get jobs. Many artists, writers, and musicians were blacklisted. In 1952, Pete Seeger was put on the blacklist. As a result, the Weavers couldn't get work. They broke up.

The impact of the folk movement was tremendous. It was at the center of the Civil Rights and antiwar protests of the 1960s and '70s. It also fueled some of the most important rock-and-roll music created by the likes of Bob Dylan, the Grateful Dead, and others.

THE YIPPIES

Throughout the 1960s, several groups continued in the tradition of the Industrial Workers of the World (IWW). These groups included the Diggers and the Youth International Party (the Yippies). They practiced a sort of intellectual syndicalism.

In the years following World War II, as many men returned home, there was a sharp rise in the birthrate. This was known as the baby boom. By the mid-1960s, many of these children, the Baby Boomers, were beginning to come of age. They were a dominant force in the population. Where the IWW attempted to radicalize the American workforce, the Diggers and the Yippies attempted to radicalize American youth.

The groups laid out philosophical programs that were similar, in some respects, to those of Charles Fourier. Freedom, they believed, was not something that was granted by the law. Freedom was something inherent in the individual. A person was free if he wanted to be. This, they believed, was the key to happiness. In some ways, they were idealistic utopians. They demanded the abolition of money, for example. They were also hardened to the political realities of the day. The Yippies, especially, engaged in constant protests. Often, they dealt explicitly with government officials.

Like the IWW, they were also profoundly persecuted. In 1968, at the Democratic National Convention in Chicago, seven Yippie leaders were arrested. They were charged with starting riots that occurred in the city's Lincoln Park. After a high-profile trial, they were convicted. Several years later, their sentences were overturned. The riots had actually been incited by police officers working on behalf of Mayor Richard Daley.

CONTEMPORARY SOCIALISM

In the 1980s, the elections of Ronald Reagan as president signified a more conservative bent to the American government, which lasted through 1993, when Democrat Bill Clinton took office. Clinton's failure to establish health care reform stalled Socialist efforts in the party. The Socialist Party of America continued to run candidates for the presidency, but with little success.

Bernie Sanders, a Democratic Socialist who ran a populist campaign for president during the 2016 election, denounced racism and the influence of rich capitalists on government.

The United States is one of the only first-world nations that does not have universal health care for its people. US government measures to provide health insurance for the elderly and poor, called Medicare and Medicaid, date to 1965. The next most sweeping change came in 2010 when President Barack Obama signed into law the Patient Protection and Affordable Care Act (PPACA), also known as Obamacare. The law, which required individuals to purchase health insurance, attempted to rein in soaring health care costs. Obamacare encountered fierce resistance from the Republican Party, and under Donald Trump's presidency, Congress attempted to repeal the law numerous times but failed. Although this effort falls considerably short of universal health care for Americans, it is a step in the direction of reform.

The 2016 presidential campaign brought self-professed Democratic Socialist Bernie Sanders to the attention of many on the political left who felt disappointed with the Democratic Party. Though Sanders eventually dropped out of the presidential race and supported Democratic candidate Hillary Clinton, his influence contributed to a growing interest in American Socialism. Since Sanders began his presidential campaign in 2015, the membership of Democratic Socialists of America has more than doubled. As the country continues to face social challenges such as illegal immigration, racism, a lack of health care, and others, Socialism may continue to gain adherents in the years to come.

1800 Robert Owen sets up model community in New Lanark, England.

1820 Charles Fourier's *Theory of Social Organization* is published.

1847 Karl Marx and Friedrich Engels write and publish *The Communist Manifesto*.

1867 Marx publishes *Das Kapital.*

1900 The British Labour Party is formed.

1917 Vladimir Lenin rises to power in Russia during the October Revolution.

1922 The Soviet Union is formed.

1923 The Frankfurt School is founded.

1928 Joseph Stalin introduces his first Five Year Plan.

1956 C. A. R. Crosland's *The Future of Socialism* is published.

1980 Howard Zinn's *A People's History of the United States* is published.

1991 The USSR collapses.

2010 Affordable Care Act (Obamacare) is established.

The Communist Manifesto by **Karl Marx**
Transcription Excerpt

The proletariat will use its political supremacy to wrest, by degree, all capital from the bourgeoisie, to centralise all instruments of production in the hands of the state, i.e., of the proletariat organised as the ruling class; and to increase the total productive forces as rapidly as possible.

These measures will, of course, be different in different countries.

Nevertheless, in most advanced countries, the following will be pretty generally applicable.

1. Abolition of property in land and application of all rents of land to public purposes.
2. A heavy progressive or graduated income tax.
3. Abolition of all rights of inheritance.
4. Confiscation of the property of all emigrants and rebels.
5. Centralisation of credit in the hands of the state, by means of a national bank with State capital and an exclusive monopoly.
6. Centralisation of the means of communication and transport in the hands of the State.
7. Extension of factories and instruments of production owned by the State; the bringing into cultivation of waste-lands, and the improvement of the soil generally in accordance with a common plan.
8. Equal liability of all to work. Establishment of industrial armies, especially for agriculture.
9. Combination of agriculture with manufacturing industries; gradual abolition of all the distinction between town and country by a more equable distribution of the populace over the country.
10. Free education for all children in public schools. Abolition of children's factory labour in its present form. Combination of education with industrial production, &c, &c.

Das Kapital by Karl Marx
Transcription Excerpt

The labour-process, turned into the process by which the capitalist consumes labour-power, exhibits two characteristic phenomena. First, the labourer works under the control of the capitalist to whom his labour belongs; the capitalist taking good care that the work is done in a proper manner, and that the means of production are used with intelligence, so that there is no unnecessary waste of raw material, and no wear and tear of the implements beyond what is necessarily caused by the work.

Secondly, the product is the property of the capitalist and not that of the labourer, its immediate producer. Suppose that a capitalist pays for a day's labour-power at its value; then the right to use that power for a day belongs to him, just as much as the right to use any other commodity, such as a horse that he has hired for the day. To the purchaser of a commodity belongs its use, and the seller of labour-power, by giving his labour, does no more, in reality, than part with the use-value that he has sold. From the instant he steps into the workshop, the use-value of his labour-power, and therefore also its use, which is labour, belongs to the capitalist. By the purchase of labour-power, the capitalist incorporates labour, as a living ferment, with the lifeless constituents of the product ...

Addendum to the minutes of Politburo [meeting] No. 93.
Transcription Excerpt

In view of the shameful collapse of grain collection in the more remote regions of Ukraine, the Council of People's Commissars and the Central Committee call upon the oblast executive committees and the oblast [party] committees as well as the raion executive committees and the raion [party] committees: to break up the sabotage of grain collection, which has been organized by kulak and counterrevolutionary elements; to liquidate the resistance of some of the rural communists, who in fact have become the leaders of the sabotage; to eliminate the passivity and complacency toward the saboteurs, incompatible with being a party member; and to ensure, with maximum speed, full and absolute compliance with the plan for grain collection.

The Council of People's Commissars and the Central Committee resolve:

To place the following villages on the black list for overt disruption of the grain collection plan and for malicious sabotage, organized by kulak and counterrevolutionary elements:

1. village of Verbka in Pavlograd raion, Dnepropetrovsk oblast.

5. village of Sviatotroitskoe in Troitsk raion, Odessa oblast.

6. village of Peski in Bashtan raion, Odessa oblast.

The following measures should be undertaken with respect to these villages :

1. Immediate cessation of delivery of goods, complete suspension of cooperative and state trade in the villages, and removal of all available goods from cooperative and state stores.

2. Full prohibition of collective farm trade for both collective farms and collective farmers, and for private farmers.

3. Cessation of any sort of credit and demand for early repayment of credit and other financial obligations.

4. Investigation and purge of all sorts of foreign and hostile elements from cooperative and state institutions, to be carried out by organs of the Workers and Peasants Inspectorate.

5. Investigation and purge of collective farms in these villages, with removal of counterrevolutionary elements and organizers of grain collection disruption.

The Council of People's Commissars and the Central Committee call upon all collective and private farmers who are honest and dedicated to Soviet rule to organize all their efforts for a merciless struggle against kulaks and their accomplices in order
to: defeat in their villages the kulak sabotage of grain collection; fulfill honestly and conscientiously their grain collection obligations to the Soviet authorities; and strengthen
collective farms.

CHAIRMAN OF THE COUNCIL OF PEOPLE'S COMMISSARS OF THE UKRAINIAN SOVIET SOCIALIST REPUBLIC - V. CHUBAR'.

SECRETARY OF THE CENTRAL COMMITTEE OF THE COMMUNIST PARTY (BOLSHEVIK) OF UKRAINE - S. KOSIOR.

6 December 1932.

BLACKLIST A list of people (often created by the government) who should be denied work because of their political or religious beliefs.

BOURGEOISIE In Marxist theory, the social class that owns the means of production.

CAPITALISM An economic system based on the private ownership of the means of production.

COMMUNISM A political system in which all property is shared by its citizens.

DIRECT DEMOCRACY A political system in which every citizen is a member of the government.

DYSTOPIA A state where everything is horrible; the opposite of a utopia.

FASCISM A kind of totalitarianism with an emphasis on extreme nationalism.

FEUDAL LORD A landowner who, in return for work, protects the farmers living on his land.

GENOCIDE A systematic elimination of a group of people based on their religious beliefs or ethnicity.

KIBBUTZ A kind of commune found primarily in Israel.

MONOPOLY A company that controls an industry with no competition.

MUCKRAKING A form of journalism designed to expose social injustices.

PHALANX A utopian community envisioned by Charles Fourier.

PROLETARIAT In Marxist theory, the working class.

SERF A farmer working on land owned by a feudal lord.

SOCIALISM A political system in which the means of production is controlled by the workers.

SYNDICALISM A political system in which workers' unions control the means of production.

TOTALITARIANISM A political system in which a single party rules without opposition.

UTOPIA An ideal state where all people live in harmony.

VILLAGIZATION A form of African Socialism in which farmers were moved from homesteads into small villages.

Canadian Museum of History
100 Laurier Street
Gatineau, QC K1A 0M8
Canada
(800) 555-5621
Website: http://www.historymuseum.ca
Facebook, Twitter, and Instagram: @CanMusHistory
The Canadian Museum of History features exhibits on the
    government and founding of Canada.

Democratic Socialists of America
75 Maiden Lane, Suite 702
New York, NY 10038
(212) 727-8610
Website: http://www.dsausa.org
Facebook and Twitter: @demsocialists
The largest Socialist organization in the United States, it works to
    support working people and reduce the role of money in politics.

Eugene V. Debs Foundation
Mailing Address:
PO Box 9454
Terre Haute, IN 47808
Museum Address:
451 N. 8th Street
Terra Haute, IN 47807
(812) 232-2163
Email: info@debsfoundation.org
Website: http://debsfoundation.org/#
Facebook: @EugeneVDebsFoundation

The organization maintains Debs's home as a museum and provides education about labor and political history.

Industrial Workers of the World
2036 West Montrose
Chicago, IL 60618-2117
Mailing address:
PO Box 180195
Chicago, IL 60618
(773) 728-0996
Email: ghq@iww.org
Website: https://www.iww.org
Facebook: @iww.org
Twitter: @_IWW
Founded in Chicago in 1905, the union seeks to demand better, fairer conditions for all workers.

International Socialist Organization
Website: https://www.internationalsocialist.org
Twitter and Instagram: @SocialistViews
The organization has chapters in many cities across the United States, including Los Angeles, Chicago, New York, and more.

Socialist Party of Canada
PO Box 31024
Victoria, BC V8N 6J3
Canada
Email: spc@worldsocialism.org
Website: http://www.worldsocialism.org/canada
Twitter: @spc_news
The party works to support workers of all types.

FOR FURTHER READING

Archer, Jules. *Extremists: Gadflies of American Society*. New York, NY: Sky Pony Press, 2017.

Bains, Alisha. *World War II.* New York, NY: Britannica Educational Publishing, 2017.

Hunter, Nick. *What Is Socialism?* Oxford, UK: Raintree, 2017.

Marriott, Emma. *Did Anything Good Come Out of World War II?* New York, NY: Rosen Publishing, 2016.

Marx, Karl, and Friedrich Engels. *The Communist Manifesto.* Minneapolis, MN: Lerner Publishing Group, 2018.

Murphy, John. *Socialism and Communism*. New York, NY: Britannica Educational Publishing, 2015.

Perkins, Anne. *Trailblazers in Politics.* New York, NY: Rosen Publishing, 2015.

Trenton, Russell. *The Russian Revolution: The Fall of the Tsars and the Rise of Communism*. New York, NY: Britannica Educational Publishing, 2016.

Uhl, Xina M., and Theodore Link. *Communism*. New York, NY: Rosen Publishing, 2019.

Zeinert, Karen. *McCarthyism and the Communist Scare in United States History.* New York, NY: Enslow Publishers, 2015.

BIBLIOGRAPHY

A+E Networks. "Che Guevara." Retrieved May 18, 2018. https://www.history.com/topics/che-guevara.

Amadeo, Kimberly. "Socialism and Its Characteristics, Pros, Cons, Examples and Types." The Balance, April 21, 2018. https://www.thebalance.com/socialism-types-pros-cons-examples-3305592.

Artifice, The. "The Rising Popularity of Dystopian Literature." April 20, 2015. https://the-artifice.com/popularity-of-dystopian-literature.

Beecher, Jonathan F. *Charles Fourier: The Visionary and His World*. Berkeley, CA: University of California Press, 1987.

Cowling, Mark, ed. *The Communist Manifesto: New Interpretations*. New York, NY: New York University Press, 1998.

Crosland, C. A. R. *The Future of Socialism*. London, UK: Jonathan Cape, 1956.

Heilbroner, Robert. "Socialism." *Concise Encyclopedia of Economics*. Retrieved on May 17, 2018. http://www.econlib.org/library/Enc/Socialism.html.

Mancini, Mark. "10 Things You Should Know About Upton Sinclair's *The Jungle*." Mental Floss, May 8, 2017. http://mentalfloss.com/article/500504/10-things-you-should-know-about-upton-sinclairs-jungle.

Marx, Karl, and Friedrich Engels. *The Marx-Engels Reader*. New York, NY: W. W. Norton & Company, 1972.

Orwell, George. *The Road to Wigan Pier*. San Diego, CA: Harcourt Brace & Co., 1958.

PBS. "Is Socialism in the United States Having a Moment?" March 27, 2017. https://www.pbs.org/newshour/politics/socialism-united-states-moment.

Renshaw, Patrick. *The Wobblies: The Story of the IWW and Syndicalism in the United States*. Chicago, IL: Ivan R. Dee, 1999.

Reuters. "Factbox: Cuba's One-Party Socialist System Among Last in World." March 11, 2018. https://www.reuters.com/article/us-cuba-election-system-factbox-factbox-cubas-one-party-socialist-system-among-last-in-world-idUSKCN1GN0QS.

Sanchez, Ray. "Venezuela: How Paradise Got Lost." CNN, July 27, 2017. https://www.cnn.com/2017/04/21/americas/venezuela-crisis-explained/index.html.

Slotnik, Daniel E. "Upton Sinclair, Whose Muckraking Changed the Meat Industry." *New York Times*, June 30, 2016. https://www.nytimes.com/interactive/projects/cp/obituaries/archives/upton-sinclair-meat-industry.

Socialist International. "I Congress of the Socialist International, Frankfurt." June 30–July 3, 1951. http://www.socialistinternational.org/viewArticle.cfm?ArticleID=39.

Thompsell, Angela. "Socialism in Africa and African Socialism." ThoughtCo., April 1, 2018. https://www.thoughtco.com/socialism-in-africa-and-african-socialism-4031311.

Wiggerhaus, Rolf. *The Frankfurt School: Its History, Theories, and Political Significance*. Cambridge, MA: MIT Press, 1994.

Zinn, Howard. *A People's History of the United States: 1492–Present*. New York, NY: Perennial Classics, 1999.

INDEX

ABOUT THE AUTHORS

Xina M. Uhl discovered her love of history while still in grade school. She went on to obtain a master of arts in history from California State University, Northridge. After teaching college-level American history, she moved into educational writing. She has authored books, textbooks, teacher's guides, lessons, and assessment questions in the field of history. When she is not writing or reading, she enjoys travel, photography, and hiking with her dogs. Her blog features her travel adventures and latest fiction projects.

Jesse Jarnow is a writer who lives in Brooklyn, New York.

PHOTO CREDITS